MW01132927

Womanrunes

A guide to their use and interpretation

Molly Remer

and Shekhinah Mountainwater

2014
Brigid's Grove
www.brigidsgrove.com

Womanrunes
A guide to their use and interpretation

First Edition 2014

ISBN-13:
978-1500761219

ISBN-10:
1500761214

Cover design, tree goddess logo, layout, and
illustrations by Mark Remer

Produced in cooperation with the estate of
Shekhinah Mountainwater (ShekhinahWorks).

*In memory of Shekhinah Mountainwater. You
inspired me and I am honored to carry on your work.*

Brigid's Grove
www.brigidsgrove.com

Listen to what is walking here
tiptoeing through your dreams
knocking at the door of your unconscious mind
whispering from shadows
calling from the full moon
twinkling in the stars
carried by the night wind woman
rising at sunset
peeking out
in tentative
yet persistent purpose.
Listen to the call
trust the talkative silence...

Contents

Introduction

Womanrunes are a unique and powerful divination system that use simple, woman-identified symbols to connect deeply with your own inner wisdom as well as the flow of womanspirit knowledge that surrounds you. Used as a personal oracle, they offer spiritual insight, understanding, and guidance as well as calls to action and discovery. Women who use them are amazed to discover how the symbols and interpretations reach out with exactly what is needed in that moment. Women's experiences with Womanrunes are powerful, magical, inspirational, potent, and mystical. The wisdom within them can be drawn upon again and again, often uncovering new information, understanding, and truth with each reading.

The simplest and most common use for Womanrunes is to draw a rune daily or when you feel an intuitive need for guidance. Draw the rune and *feel* into it. What is it sharing with you? Read the companion interpretation and let it soak in. These symbols speak to something deep within you. You may have the experience of feeling *heard* and *answered* when you choose a rune and read its interpretation.

Womanrunes provide a pathway to your own "truth-sense." They open you up to your own internal guidance and to messages and inspiration from the Goddess, the Earth, or your spiritual guides.

Womanrunes may also be used to do guidance readings for friends or clients. Messages from Womanrunes are not prescriptive or directive, instead they serve as a rich conduit to exactly what you need to hear and receive in that moment.

Many women also find it satisfying to draw or carve Womanrunes onto art, calendars, sculptures and more. Used in this way, Womanrunes can attract their messages deeply into your life or can serve as potent declarations of intention.

Why Such Simple Images?

Many divination and oracle systems include beautiful artwork on the cards. Womanrunes are simple symbols and are, in fact, a type of symbol "writing" that speaks to a deep part of the soul. The clean focus and simplicity of the Womanrunes symbols evoke rich messages and soul guidance in their own special way that differs from the image-rich paintings of other systems. They are also very easy to use directly yourself—including them in your own art, drawing or etching them onto objects, and thereby writing them into your consciousness in a *living* manner. Used as a dynamic, hands-on, participatory system,

Womanrunes become part of your own language of the Divine, the Goddess, your inner wisdom, and womanspirit truths.

About Shekhinah Mountainwater

Make for yourself a power spot
Bring you a spoon and a cooking pot
Bring air
Bring fire
Bring water
Bring earth
And a new universe you will birth...
–Shekhinah Mountainwater in The Goddess Celebrates by Diane Stein

I was interested in Goddess spirituality for many years before eventually discovering Shekhinah Mountainwater. When I did, she'd already passed away. I bought a used copy of her book *Ariadne's Thread* and fell in love with it. I learned about her Womanrunes and fell in love with them even more. In the book I quote above, Shehkinah describes herself in this way:

"...I have taken vows to be a full-time priestess and Goddess-worker. I teach classes, make ceremony, develop calendars and culture, write, play music, create art and poetry. I long for a society where women and men are free to be themselves, to be creative and loving and fulfilled in all their great potential..." (p. 86)

Shekhinah was a foremother of Goddess spirituality and discovered the Goddess in the early 1970's. She began teaching, writing, and singing with an emphasis on women's spirituality and worked as a priestess with women's circles from the 1970's until her death in 2007.

In Shekhinah's own words in her classic book *Ariadne's Thread:*

> "I am a lover, a mother, a daughter, and a sister of women. I am a priestess, a teacher, a writer, an artist, a scholar, a musician, tarot and runemaker, reader of tarot and runes, a craftswoman, a ritualist, a healer, and a changer. I am a wild and watery woman, a magical mystical poet...a weaver of song and myth. I am a founding mother of the women's spirituality movement, one of the first to channel Goddess revolution in our times" (p. 380).

About Womanrunes

She weave
She spin
She gather, she
The morning
Noon
And night of me
Budding spring
And swelling summer
Chilling winter
Weaveth she
Up and outer
Down and inner
Weave and gather
Silent spinner
Spider woman
Spinning three
Timeless times
Of destiny...
(Shekhinah Mountainwater, *Ariadne's Thread*, p. 207)

Runes are a type of magical writing or magical
alphabet system used for divination,
communication, and understanding of self and
cosmos. The most commonly seen runes today
derive from old Celtic runes of Europe. Some
evidence indicates that these were first invented
and used by women, possibly gifted to them by the
Norns, the three Goddesses of Fate. They are also

associated with the God Odin.

The Birth of Womanrunes

Womanrunes are a system of forty-one female-identified symbols for divination, self-development, and personal growth. They were created by Shekhinah Mountainwater in 1987 and introduced in her book *Ariadne's Thread* in 1991.

In 1987 after having worked with traditional runes, but sensing "something more" behind them, Shekhinah's friend suggested she create a specifically woman-identified rune system. On the Summer Solstice of that year, Shekhinah explains, "goddess-lightning struck. I fell into a state of enchantment and, in a single day, the symbols for my Womanrunes were born... Suddenly I was liberated, and the new symbols poured out beneath my pen. Like the priestesses of old, I opened myself, and the Goddess sent me Her magic" (p. 219).

In 2012, I was reading a back issue of SageWoman magazine from 1988 and stumbled across an article about Womanrunes. I instantly fell in love with them. They issued a powerful call to me. I scoured the internet for more information, where I eventually found a handout and pronunciation guide (reprinted on page 126). I purchased Shekhinah's book, *Ariadne's Thread*, and began making Womanrunes sets at women's spirituality retreats with my friends.

As a priestess and ritual facilitator, I shared the basic list of Womanrunes with my women's circle and we adopted them as a special part of our group, using them on a variety of group projects. Shekhinah's book, *Ariadne's Thread*, explains that Womanrunes are very intuitive and can readily be interpreted using your own inherent sense of their meanings. However, I also observed that many women wished for additional explanations of each rune beyond Shekhinah's original titles and associated words.

The depth of my connection to the symbols led me to begin to develop more extensive interpretations of the meaning of each rune. I began a personal practice of drawing one rune and then going to a sacred place in the woods with it to see what it had to tell me. Using this process I created a developed interpretation of the meaning of each rune.

Accessing Our Truth-Sense

In the book *Runes of the Goddess,* author PMH Atwater uses a set of 16 runes based on the ancient Elder Futhark runes and she calls them Goddess runes. With regard to the significance and meaning of runes as a divination systems, she explains:

"*Runic symbols are not magic in and of themselves.*

Symbols are illustrative, not directive. The magic comes from the way they stimulate feelings, emotions, and memories in the one who uses them. Forgotten wisdoms hidden within the psyche begin to awaken and resurface. This is the real magic... uncovering the deeper depths of your own being." (p. 24)

She goes on to explain:

"Learning the way of a cast utilizes sacred play to help you step into your own 'dream' (the life you live) so you can view issues from another perspective. This enables you to develop an ongoing pathway into the heart and soul of your 'truth-sense,' that intuitive wellspring at the central core of all that you are. Once the pathway is developed, you can almost magically move beyond sacred play into a kind of 'flow' state where 'moment matches mind.' This is synchronicity— where random events cease to be random, and seemingly unrelated things link together in meaningful and wonderful ways." (p. 26)

This is what I experienced in the woods with the Womanrunes: a pathway to my own "truth-sense." Atwater's description of how she first saw and connected with these runes reminds me of my own experience with the Womanrunes. They called to me and spoke to me in ways I am still exploring.

With Shekhinah's Womanrunes, I felt an irresistible intuitive connection at first contact, but I needed something *more* than their original one to three word descriptions. My friends, too, expressed this need. We made runesets together and they said, *"now what? How do we actually read and use these? We need more!"* In what eventually became a year-long project, I began deepening into the meaning of each rune individually while alone in a sacred place in the woods and writing an interpretation based on this intuitive information.

The Runes

0:	◯	The Circle.	*Rune of the Self.*
1:	⌂	The Witch's Hat.	*Rune of Magic.*
2:	☾	The Crescent Moon.	*Rune of Divination.*
3:	▽	The Yoni.	*Rune of Making.*
4:	ﻥ	The Flame.	*Rune of Fire.*
5:	♡	The Heart.	*Rune of Love.*
6:	⚒	The Labyris.	*Rune of Will.*
7:	⚨	The Dancing Woman.	*Rune of Power.*
8:	▢	The Box.	*Rune of Boundaries.*
9:	⬤	The Dark Moon.	*Rune of Wisdom.*
10:	☯	The Wheel.	*Rune of Fate.*
11:	⌐	The Pendulum.	*Rune of Karma.*
12:	⊖	The Reflection.	*Rune of Surrender.*
13:	⚲	The Flying Woman.	*Rune of Transformation.*
14:	⚱	The Cauldron.	*Rune of Alchemy.*
15:	◗	The Whole Moon.	*Rune of Psyche.*
16:	⚮	The Serpent.	*Rune of Awakening.*
17:	⛤	The Moon and Star.	*Rune of Faith.*

18:		The Sun.	Rune of Healing.
19:		The Dancing Women.	Rune of Celebration.
20:		The Great Wheel.	Rune of Infinity.
21:		The Egg.	Rune of Naming.
22:		The Sisters.	Rune of Friendship.
23:		The Seed.	Rune of Waiting.
24:		The Tool.	Rune of Labor.
25:		The Winged Circle.	Rune of Freedom.
26:		The Cauldron of Reflection.	Rune of Solitude.
27:		The Crowned Heart.	Rune of Unconditional Love.
28:		The Tree.	Rune of Prosperity.
29:		The Pentacle.	Rune of Protection.
30:		The Two Circles.	Rune of Merging.
31:		The Two Triangles.	Rune of Focus.
32:		Moonboat.	Rune of Journeys.
33:		The Hearth.	Rune of Nurturance.
34:		The Cauldron of Dancing Women.	Rune of Honor.

35:	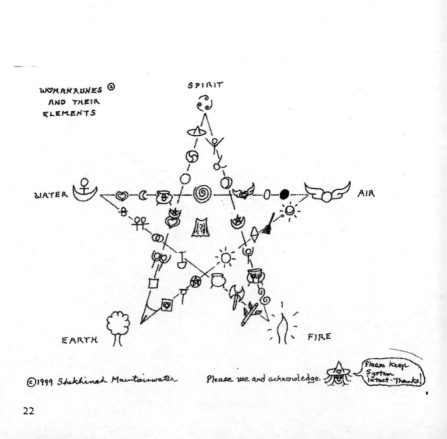	The Broom.	*Rune of Purification.*
36:		The Spiral.	*Rune of Initiation.*
37:		The Wand.	*Rune of Blessing.*
38:		The Sun and Moon.	*Rune of Laughter.*
39:		The Winged Heart.	*Rune of Ecstasy.*
40:		The Veil.	*Rune of Mystery.*

WOMANRUNES AND THEIR ELEMENTS

SPIRIT

WATER

AIR

EARTH

FIRE

©1999 Shekhinah Mountainwater   Please use and acknowledge.   Please keep system intact - Thanks!

Interpretations

o: The Circle.

Rune of the Self. Beginnings. Potential. Innocence.

The truth of *being* may be grander and deeper and broader than you can ever imagine. Look before you and bear witness to the magic, the pure potentiality that surrounds you all the time. Is not your very Self a true *miracle?* Thinking, breathing, moving, walking, grasping, laughing, loving, writing, talking, holding, birthing, creating. These systems that animate your body, beat your heart, grow your fingernails, circulate your blood, digest your food, gaze at your baby. This is *incredible.* Incredibly majestic, incredibly miraculous, and incredibly mysterious.

What is this process of cell division? What is this process of thought? What is this process of life and living? Where does it come from and where does it go? How does it work? *Really work.* The language of meiosis and mitosis and synapses and electrical impulses is not enough. We can explain life in scientific terms... but underlying it is still a fundamental majesty of unimaginable wonder.

Just as the acorn holds limitless oaks, the Self has limitless potential. Expanding, contracting, opening, closing, leaping, pausing, watching, knowing, asking questions...

Pause and witness the miracle.

1: The Witch's Hat.

Rune of Magic. Spells. Enchantment.

This is a rune of naming and claiming and owning and doing. This is a rune of creation, of webweaving, spellcasting, and magicmaking. This is rune of celebration and of *showing up*. What have you been afraid to claim? What name have you been afraid to speak? What scares you to step forward and own?

We all have magic within us, boiling in our cauldron of being. Keeping time with our heartsong, crackling out through our fingertips, waiting to be expressed and sung into being. What enchants you? What needs your sparkle and spice? What needs your magic? What spell are you casting? Is it a conscious one? One with purpose, intention, and focus? Or is it unconscious and still forming?

Is it time to sweep off the hat and step forward bold and proud? Or is it time to scoop it up and put it on saying, "This is me. This is who I am." You are capable, you are creative, you are alive. You are the enchantress. You are magic. Gather up your resources. Collect your attention. Stir up your power. Step forth with boldness.

This is me. A magical woman. And, yes, that pointed hat is mine.

2: The Crescent Moon.

Rune of Divination. Ritual. Door to Unconscious.

The Moon Mother calls you. She dances around the edges of your conscious awareness, singing your name, tugging at your spirit. Listen to the Dreamtime...

What is knocking at the doorway of your soul?
What calls to you in the night?
Are you dreaming?
Have you given up on dreams?
Are you listening?
Have you stopped trying?
Do you remember your dreams?
Do you heed their messages?

The Goddess speaks in the language of dreamtime, from deep, dark places and in fuzzy, sleepy awareness. Tune in, look inside, wait for wisdom. It wants to enter, it's on its way. Carried by the moon, drifting in starlight, singing to you, drawing you near. Moon Mother, Dream Mother. Winds of change and destiny are swirling.

Pay attention, take heed, become conscious. In the seemingly coincidental connections and links of life your unconscious, your deep self is speaking to you. She knows many things.

Divination is not about predicting the future, but about understanding your path and heeding the guidance laid out before you in many bright, sparkling, starry, and shadowy ways. She speaks in dreams, speaks in nudges, speaks in signs, signals, synchronicities. This is the language of symbol, myth, pattern, and magic.

This rune also reminds us of the power of ritual. Of gathering together with intention and purpose and power, of raising energy, of sealing bonds, of linking arms in sisterhood and circle and solidarity. This rune calls upon you to create your own magic, to define your own truths, and to stir your own rituals into communal meaning.

You can do it. You already know how.

3: The Yoni.

Rune of Making. Creativity. Fertility. Wealth. Pleasure. Birth.

This is a rune of creation. The womb of all possibility and all changes. The cauldron of life. Doorway, initiation, birth, and re-birth. Receptive, open, embracing. Fertile in her power and her purpose. What waits within to be given birth and what wants to enter to incubate? What nestles in fertile ground?

This is a hopeful rune, a joyful rune. One that reminds us to dance in the moonlight, to enjoy being naked, to delight in our bodies, and to celebrate the bodies, capacities and creations of others. This is rune of form. Of being formed. Of forming. This is a rune of fertile possibility.

Put your hand on your belly. What is waiting there in your pelvic bowl? What is waiting in quiet wombspace? What is hidden away, but growing bigger and bigger and waiting to be born? What do you need and what needs you?

Take it to the body, bring it down into your pelvis. Sweep around the curve of the pelvic bowl and *listen*. What does she want to tell you?

There is a time to nurture and a time to be nurtured. A time to make and create. A time to receive and wait. Take pleasure in being alive at this moment. Take pleasure in the works of your hands and the sweetness of kisses upon your lips. Enjoy, stroke, touch, feel, engage. Honor feeling. Scoop it all up. Run wild with life, breathe deep, and smile.

Something is building to a climax and ecstasy awaits.

4: The Flame.

Rune of Fire. Energy. Vitality. Enthusiasm. Amazon.

When you draw this rune, rest assured that *you can do it.* It is time to draw upon your deep, fiery, inner resolve. Let yourself ignite. Approach your task with enthusiasm and vitality. If that which you must do is not serving your vitality, either *do not do it,* or find a way to light its fire. Call upon your warrior, call upon your Amazon spirit. Step forth boldly, go forth with grand gestures and resolute purpose. At the same time, *dance.* Put on your tribal paint. Adorn your head and body. Dance with your inner fire. Dance with your vision. Dance with your purpose.

Your enthusiasm is what keeps you going. Your energy is what brightens the world around you. Your fire is that which rests within.

It is hot, it is holy, and it feeds you.

5: The Heart.

Rune of Love. Passion.

Right here, right now, *pause.* Rest, and know, that you are *so loved.* Held in love, supported in love, grounded in love. Draw it up. Draw it in. Breathe easy. You need not *do* anything. When you draw this rune, take a moment to acknowledge how often you act from a place of deep love. How underneath the surface of hurry and frustration and worry, there is a deep wellspring of love that drives you. And, in the next moment, extend your awareness, your grace and compassion, to recognize how often those around also act from deep love. Love as the ground of being, love as the field of being. This love underlies your living and your interactions. Trust it, know it, be it. It is *inexhaustible.* It sustains you.

Heart-centered, breathing easy, step forward with courage, resilience, ease, and self-acceptance. This rune is also about love of **life**, that which is right in front of you, unfolding every day. This is *it*, this is real. Don't argue with reality!

The Love rune also reminds you to take a turn to *receive*, to be nurtured, to draw in the love of those around you, to share passion, to remember to laugh. You can receive, you can give. Both capacities are boundless. Walk in love and love will continue to rise up to greet you.

Passion. It bubbles. It boils. It dances and sings. It enlivens your spirit, it animates you. Passion. Juice. Energy. Roll in it, roll with it. Say yes. Drink it up. Laugh, revel, celebrate, create, harmonize.

Passion is the elixir of being and it speaks from the heart. Threading through your veins, beating in your chest, lightening your footsteps.

Embrace it and *smile*.

6: The Labyris.

Rune of Will. Power in the world. Mobility. Having one's way.

This is a rune of assertiveness. Of standing up for oneself. Of claiming unapologetically one's place on the planet and in the stream of life. This is a strong rune, a steady rune, a rune you draw when the time has come to make decisions. When the time has come to say no. When the time has come to *choose*.

It is a rune of action, determination, energy, sustenance, vitality, and truth. It reminds us that it is necessary to speak up. To do what must be done. To say yes and to say no, without explaining, justifying, rationalizing or apologizing. The Universe is made up of many wills. Many wills joining, bumping into one another, dominating, submitting, sharing, giving up, being stubborn. The Labyris rune is about a strong, steady, inner will. A sense of personal power and the ability to stand in that personal power. The ability to step forward with purpose. To speak up with firmness. It is not about dominating or oppressing or submerging the wills of others. It can remind us of the power in partnership, in collaboration. Of the power found in working together, while still asserting one's own self-responsibility, potency and personal power.

This rune turns up when it is time to make changes.

The time has come to draw upon your flexibility and your ability to notice what needs to be different, what is calling out for action and change, and to dig deep for the courage and will that are necessary to enact those changes. Remember that mobility can sometimes involve knowing when to *wait*. When to be still and when to return to something later in one's life course. This is a stubborn rune. It wants its own way. You want your own way. It isn't wrong to want that.

Have you been silent for too long? Have you squelched your own desires? Have you pretended to be something you are not? Have you expected others to read your mind and meet your needs for you, without needing to speak up? Have you been wanting to flee? Have you been wanting to quit or say no, but don't know how? That's where this double-headed axe comes in. *It can cut both ways.*

What needs to be pruned away? Watch out. She's chopping there. Be careful not to cut the ones you love, to cut off more than you bargained for or more than you want. Handle blades with care, for they can be dangerous. Is this what you worry about in asserting your own will? That you are dangerous? That people do not get what they need from you? That you are not enough? You are *more* than enough and sometimes that is scary. And, sometimes it scares others.

Slice cleanly and without apology. Slice carefully and without regret. Remember to keep enough room around you to swing the blade freely.

7: The Dancing Woman.

Rune of Power. Power from within. Strength.

Can you step into your personal power? Can you stand in your personal power? Do you know how it feels to do so? How does it look? How does it taste? What do you feel ripple through you? How do you know that you're there? Standing in power. Power in standing. Interstanding. Understanding. Steady. Firm. Self-aware. Self-committed. Purposeful. Potent. Powerful.

There is nothing somber or apologetic about this rune. It is unabashedly exuberant and confident and gracefully complete, totally alive. Perhaps standing in your power is what you need. But, perhaps *dancing* in your power is possible too. Singing in your power. Holding your power. *Being* your power. Inhabiting your power. Celebrating your body with abandon. Celebrating your mind and personality with the same. Honoring your quirks, finding compassion within you that stretches around you and out into the world.

It starts within. It builds within. Then, it crests in a peak that ripples outward, impacting all who you encounter and inspiring them too: to step into their power. To stand in their power. To dance in their power. Power shared does not diminish, it expands, until each person can sing her own true song, drum her own rhythm, and dance for the heck of it.

Stretch your arms wide, open them to the sky, swoop them down and touch the earth. Feel it there within you. **You are a powerful woman.**

Draw it up, draw it down, draw it in.

Breathe with absolute certainty and clarity that who you are is *powerfully enough.*

8: The Box

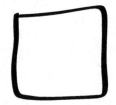

Rune of Boundaries. Limitation. Stability. Lessons.

Boundaries. Hemmed in. Closed off. Boxed off. **Or:** safe, protected, assertive. How do you need to stand up for yourself? What do you need to speak out about? How do you own your own needs? How do you respect your own inner call? What do you want to do? How do you want to spend your time?

The Box reminds us of the critical importance of saying NO and how that relates to our ability to stay alive, vibrant, connected, and *vital.* In order to be of good service, in order to be strong and healthy, sometimes we will disappoint others, let them down, say no to good ideas, good projects, and even sometimes to legitimate requests for help. What does your body want from you? What does your soul want from you? What do you need? *Heed that call.*

Set firm boundaries, establish personal space, draw lines in the sand if needed. Mothers know, women know, that boundaries must also be fluid and flexible, because that which cannot yield when necessary, snaps and breaks. Make sure that in your effort not to become taken advantage of, you do not become shut off, boxed in, and unable to connect.

We must forever balance the forces of separation and connection. Boundaries.

Boundaries. Lines. Squares. Diamonds. Protective forces. Sometimes with sharp edges. Sometimes with assertive language, but blessedly essential to wholeness of being and defragmentation of self. Sometimes we desperately need The Box. And, so we refine these boundaries, hone them, trust them, own them, and respect them, in ourselves and in others, when that is what our lives call out for.

The time has come to draw firm lines.

9: The Dark Moon.

Rune of Wisdom. Door to the unknown. Crone's rune.

This is a foggy rune, a mysterious rune, a dark and knowing rune. This is the rune that holds questions that you're still learning how to ask. This is the rune that waits behind the veil. This is a rune of digging deeper, of twisting harder, and of asking more complicated *and* more simple questions and of being willing to wait in darkness for the reply.

This is a rune of honesty and truth-telling and truth-speaking and wisdom sharing, but it is also a rune that accepts fuzzy boundaries and imperfect and unclear understandings. It is a rune that recognizes limitations and honors rest. It gives permission for *not knowing*. It holds both. The speaking of your wisdom and the floundering in the darkness and confusion of your unknowing. It is the recognizing that wisdom comes in knowing how to ask the questions, not in always having all the answers. It is the rune of the wise woman, the sage, the crone, the ancient mother, the ancestral mother, the dark goddess, the deep within.

What do you know that you don't know? What secrets are you keeping? What is waiting to be brought from behind the veil? What is content to remain shrouded in silent mystery and phenomenal, wild grace?

As I wrote this interpretation, I looked up and came suddenly eye to eye with a hawk in the forest for the first time...

You never know what is watching you from silent wings and shadowed, wild spaces.

10: The Wheel.

Rune of Fate. Change of Fortune.

What crackles in the leaves right under your feet? What stirs amidst the stones? What pushes up from cracked earth? What is bathed in the river? What cautiously creeps into the sunlight? What waits until the moon has risen to bloom?

Destiny, fate, fortune. You are not in complete control. You do not make all the choices. A million factors, seen and unseen, have gone into the unfolding spiral of your life and will continue to co-create it. You are a thread in the tapestry, a note in the song, a star in the sky, a drop in the ocean, a leaf on the tree, a cell in the body, a pattern in the sand. But, somewhere in the stars, your name is written and a sound chimes only for you. The tracing of your veins, the patterns of your fingertips, the gene patterns of your soulbeing. Is this fate? Is this destiny? Is this you?

You are woven by the weaver of all that is, held in the great, grand web of incarnation that encompasses time and space and everything beyond. The wheel turns, life unfolds, your breath moves in and out.

You are wild, wise, and wonderful. Don't waste what you've been given. Don't wait to play your music.

Don't wait. Roll. Roll with the wheel

11: The Pendulum.

Rune of Karma. Justice. Ethics. Trust. Conscience. Old Patterns.

Stop making bargains with life, with yourself, with the divine, and let the pattern unfold and the rhythm emerge. What once was will be. What will be, will be. What is, *is*. It has been said that the arc of the universe is long and bends towards justice. Root yourself in an ethic of care. Trust that as the pendulum swings, tick-tock, tick-tock, it will eventually return to partnership, cooperation, and love.

You know you can trust yourself to do what is right. You know you can trust your own conscience and the rhythm of your own heart.

Which way is the pendulum of your own life swinging right now? Is it bending towards justice? Is it rooted in care? Do the outward expressions of your being reflect your deepest and truest values? Are you walking your talk? Are you living what you claim to desire? Are you doing it? Are you doing this work? Are you *being it*? Can you allow yourself? Can you give yourself permission?

Take a deep breath. Open your hands. Drop your shoulders. Release your brow. Feel yourself planted on the earth in this moment. Then, ask yourself: *what do I know to be true?* In and out. In and out. Thrum, thrum, thrum. You can hear it.

Pay attention. She's talking to you. Are you listening?

12: The Reflection.

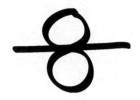

Rune of Surrender. Gentleness. Sacrifice. Letting go.

It isn't all up to you. Sometimes you have to step back and just let it unfold. Sometimes you have to bob in the current. Sometimes you have to crest with the waves. Sometimes you have to get battered against the shore, ground up into something finely textured and soft. Surrender isn't permanent. It is just part of discernment. When to hold, when to fold. When to stop, when to go. When to plant, when to harvest. When to say yes, and when to say no.

This is a rune of open heart and open hands. This is a rune of acceptance and yielding. This is a rune of opening and releasing. This is a rune of letting yourself float, to be carried by unseen forces, rather than wrestling for and with control. Sometimes it is okay to go where the wind takes you, to drift with the current, to float out to sea, to give up and to be okay with it. Pay attention. What is asking you to let go? What is wanting to be freed? What is offering itself up to be sacrificed? What is waiting for you to unclench your fists and go with the flow?

Somewhere in the quiet stillness of your own breath are the answers that you seek, the wisdom that you hold, and the knowing that is eternal. Unclench your fist. Unclench your life. Release, release. Let go and *float*. Smooth your brow, close your eyes. Inhale. Exhale.

Soften into the gentleness that surrounds you.

13: The Flying Woman.

Rune of Transformation. Death and Rebirth. Shapeshifting and change.

Becoming, becoming, becoming. Transforming, transforming, transforming. Unearthing, unearthing, unearthing. Being reborn, again and again. Isn't transformation the very *work of being*? The very work of the soul? The very fabric of thealogy, community, sisterhood, friendship, relationship, and personhood. Transformation: the core of life, the purpose of being.

What does *becoming* mean to you? Let it never mean you are somehow less than whole in this very moment. Each breath you take is a transformation. Each morning that dawns, holds the promise of rebirth. Each stone you flip, each page you turn, each word you type, it is all part of the fabric of transforming, becoming, changing. Change is constant. Sometimes change is scary and unwelcome. Sometimes you want to jump up and dance naked with it in the moonlight. You may want to hold on, to cling to something permanent, but the only thing that is really permanent is that unfolding, unwinding, deconstructing, deconstricting, unclenching, releasing.

Let go, so you can watch what emerges. You can dance with her, sing with her, fly with her, cry with her, resist her, ignore her, embrace her, become her. *The Flying Woman.* She's ready to go. Are you ready? Can you flow with the tide and ebb with the moon? Dance at the edge of pain? Howl with potential? Respond to the rhythm played by your heart?

Join hands with your sisters, stretch out glad arms to the children, and then spin...

Spin together, in this beautiful, glorious, terrifying, magnificent, exhilarating, exhausting, amazingly eternal dance of life--in time, in space, in love.

14: The Cauldron.

*Rune of Alchemy. Temperance. Centeredness.
Discipline. Art. Containment.*

This rune is a rune to turn to when you don't know exactly what to do. Take it to the cauldron, stir it up, let it bubble, let it boil, let it percolate, let it stew, let it meld together with its companions until it emerges as something richer, deeper, more complex and flavorful than what originally went into the pot. Let it cook until you taste with spicy certainty exactly what has called your name, what awaits your flame, what sings your song, and what strums your heart.

The cauldron holds a promise, it holds potential, and it holds that which you are already cooking. This is a rune of alchemy and transformation. What pieces are you holding? What can you contribute to the greater whole? What can you share with others? What flavor do you add to the mix? Bring it. Show up. Be counted. Do not be afraid to share.

This is a rune of focus and discipline, of centering

yourself deep within your body, of taking your thoughts down out of the mind and into your pelvis instead. What is she telling you? What does she want? What does she need? What does she know?

When you receive this rune, something is waiting to be blended. Something is waiting to be dished up, something is waiting to be offered. Something is waiting to be created. You are the container for the emerging brew. *Get ready for the feast.*

Hold your promise over hot coals and watch it bubble into life.

15: The Whole Moon.

Rune of Psyche. Moon Energy and Mysteries. Cycles.

Cycles of life. Cycles of living. Cycles of love. Cycles of friendships. Changes. Growth. Some things blossom in the moonlight. Some things quietly curl up and retreat. Hope knows the mystery of the night. Our hearts know the mystery too. When we try to speak it out loud, it is slippery and undefinable. This is a rune both of paradox and change. Growth and decline. Effort, possibility, potential, and surprise. What mysteries are waiting for you in the light of the moon? What mysteries are waiting for you in the dark of the moon? What wants to be illuminated? What wants to hide? What wants to grow? What wants to decline?

Watch for the thin sliver of a fresh idea. Watch, too, for the fading crescent of that which has run its course. Reach out your arms to the mystery. Stretch them as a wide as you can. Stretch yourself as wide as you can. And, even then, know with joy that you can *never* embrace it all. This vastness. This void. This grandeur. This dramatic sweep of time and place and power.

Hold on. She ebbs and flows. The rest of life matches the tug of the moon. New things cresting, building, towering, standing tall. Then, crashing against the shore, pulling back, fading away, gathering strength and courage, and returning again and again.

It is time to listen to the whispers of your body as she is tugged to dance in the light of the moon.

16: The Serpent.

Rune of Awakening. Kundalini energy. Cataclysm.
Shattering.

Something has awoken, something has arisen,
something is coming. Prepare for impact. Your
world will be shaken and you will emerge anew
from the splinters, like the phoenix. Shattered, tat-
tered, torn away, splintered, crushed, broken. And
yet, **there**. What's that? Something rises. Something with glittering eyes. Something with clarity of
focus and vision and purpose and power. Something undulating, dancing in the rubble, climbing
from the wreckage, lifting up joyful arms and open
hands and saying: I'm ready. *Here I am!*

Shakti. Kundalini. This energy that coils at the base
of your spine and unfurls through your throat and
out your fingertips. *That.* That power, that vibrance,
that potent aliveness. That elixir of courage. It lives
in you. It walks with you. It waits with you to be un-
leashed, unfurled, spread wide, ignited. What within you is ready to awaken? What around you is
ready to awaken? What are you are *not seeing*?

What have you been purposefully not looking at? It is time to meet her eyes. To taste her breath of freedom and to join with her in a serpertine dance of cataclysmic awakening and surrender.

Welcome, Shakti. We are ready for your shaking. We are ready to be cracked open.

We are ready to rise.

17: The Moon and Star.

Rune of Faith. Inspiration. Truth. Psychic Healing.

Hold to the hope. Hold to the vision. Hold to the healing. Hold to the vigil kept by your heart.

What do you have faith in? What does faith mean anyway? What do you know to be true? Where do you find inspiration and sacred calling? What fire is waiting to be lit within your own breast, your own home, your own community?

What do you have to share? What do you have to say?

Sing about it. Dance about it. Tell about it. Engage in deep talk. Deep thought. Deep commitment. Deep change. Deep healing.

This is a rune of uncovering. Of revealing. A rune of tapping in to that which already is, to that which you already are. To the potential that waits in your heart to bloom. To the passion that waits in your throat to be loosed. For the fire of creativity that swirls in your belly to be freed. Rune of inspiration. Rune of igniting.

Have faith in your own deep purpose, your own deep potential, your own deep calling, your own deep longing. Be still. Place your hand on your heart and *listen*. The answers wait within.

The sun rises, the earth turns, the moon bathes the world, the tides lap the shore. We are carried by a great wind across the sky. We are a vital thread in the weaving of Life. An intricate and interesting part of a magnificent tapestry of Being in which it becomes difficult to distinguish weaver, web, and thread, so closely are they wound together.

After you've spent time in your own heart space, *open your eyes*. Take a look around, gaze at this bright, beautiful, wonderful world. Look at the smiles of those you love. Look at the memories that have carved space in your heart. Feel what comes welling up out of you. What must be said. This is your truth. This is your inspiration. This is your healing. It is also your gift.

May the moon and stars always light your way, for you carry stardust in your bones, and some part of you will soar on the wings of time forever.

18: The Sun.

Rune of Healing. Rejuvenation. Recreation. Play. Radiance.

When you draw this rune, you know the time has come to be healed. Not healing as in forgetting, or in letting go, but in accepting, opening, changing, and growing. An integration of difficult changes you may have experienced in life. Healing may be physical, it may be emotional, it may be spiritual, it may be relational. Consider in which ways you need healing and rejuvenation. In interpersonal relationships? Physical health? Emotional well-being? Mental health? In your relationship with yourself? In your relationship with your body and with the earth?

Healing is both **possible** in all there is and **available** through all there is. Healing comes in sharing silences, and sharing stories, and in sharing songs. Healing comes in creation, in offering to others, in opening your heart to a circle of women, in silence with another, in connection with your partner. It is also found in being playful and laughing together.

This rune also reminds us that **trying again** is always worthwhile. Draw upon the resources of the earth. Draw upon the resources of your sister. Draw upon the resources of your own heart.

In quiet spaces and laughing faces, *you will be healed.*

19: The Dancing Women.

*Rune of Celebration. Community. Shared power.
Solidarity.*

When you come together with your sisters,
anything is possible. When you join with others in
community, you can move mountains. You can build
bridges and you can drum by the fire. When you
listen to each other deeply, you come to know and
be known, to understand and to be understood, to
hear and be heard, to see and be seen. You are not
alone. You are not isolated. There is a power in
cooperation, power in joining hands, of linking
arms, of connecting hearts, and forging paths
together. Shaping lives in concert with one another.

Power expands when it is shared, it is not
something that is in finite supply or that can be
distributed by any one person. Power is within us
and we must step out and into it, owning our own
power, *inhabiting* our own power; fully and without
apology, with grace and with firmness and trust.

When people come together, each standing in their

own power, the power base multiplies and becomes infinitely possible. Many hands make light work, many voices make one song, many hearts beat together, many people stand strong.

This is a rune of uniting, of togetherness, of working, laughing, playing, celebrating, and journeying, with a shared focus.

There need not already be a path; walking together we create one.

20: The Great Wheel.

Rune of Infinity. Completion. Wholeness. Universality.

Circularity. Wholeness. That which you seek can be found within you. And, in reaching out to those around you. Spaces, people, opportunities, deeds. It is *right there*, you need only look at it.

Round, curving destiny. Rough carved shape of being. Patterns hewn in places and people, speaking the language of community. You have what you need. You are what you seek.

The wheel spins, the world turns, the pattern weaves, your heart beats.

Your place is here, in the infinite spiral of life.

21: The Egg.

Rune of Naming. Word of Power. Magic Naming. Communication.

This is a rune of identification. This is a rune of differentiation. This is a rune of owning. Who are you? What do you know? What do you have to offer? What do you have to give? Own it. Do it. Be it. Try it. Say it. Know it.

Naming takes courage. Speaking takes truth. Story-sharing takes depth of being and clear vision.

This is a rune of communication, clarity in word, thought, and deed. It is hopeful, it is helpful, it is magical, it is purposeful, it is conscious, *it is so*. Listen to the world around you, speak words of power, ask for the magic names of the things that surround you. Listen deeply for answers to questions you didn't know you were asking, for perspectives you didn't know you needed, and for support and acknowledgement.

You will be heard in unexpected places, in unexpected ways, with unexpected allies, of time, place, heart, truth, and being.

22: The Sisters.

Rune of Friendship. Sisterhood. Bonding. Promises and vows.

Reach out your hand to your sister, she's reaching back. Fingers touch in a moment of solidarity and suddenly you know that you have never been alone.

This friendship is ancient, wise, and deep and it crosses boundaries of time, space, culture, tradition, values and becomes part of the fabric of something eternal that women have been weaving since the first woman took the first breath. Some sisters come and some sisters go, some become entwined with you so that your paths and destinies intersect permanently in an unfolding spiral of becoming, exploring, learning, and knowing together.

This rune calls you to circle with your sisters, it calls you to gather the women, it calls you to drum, to dance and to sing together. It calls you to make ceremony and ritual and magic and celebration together. It calls you to comb out her hair, to place a crown of flowers in her hair, to wash her feet with love, to cry with her, to laugh with her, to sing with her, to celebrate her, and yourself and yourselves together. It calls you to make eye contact, to see her, to really see her, and to say, "I hear you, I hear you. Message received."

When you promise to be true to a friendship, you are promising to be true to yourself, as a woman on this earth. When you create ritual together, you are creating a microcosm of what could be, of what can be, of what is possible, and you are giving birth to what women's relationships and friendships can look like: whole, healthy, strong, accepting, supportive, honest, authentic, graceful, and real.

Keep your eyes open, look for her. Don't be afraid to offer an invitation, a shoulder, a hand, or a song. Let her know she's welcome, let her know you're safe, let her know you're willing to birth something new together. Invite her in. Ask her to stay. Make her tea. Say thank you. And, be open to receive. Remember that relationships are reciprocal and you can give in healthy ways to each other.

This cord of sisterhood is eternal and strong, but it requires attention, dedication, honesty, and power to continue weaving the strands into deeper, more authentic connection and trust.

Listen, she calls your name. Go dance with her, barefoot in the sand.

23: The Seed.

Rune of Waiting. Ripening. Pregnancy. Assessment.

Something waits beneath the surface of your life. If you listen, if you're quiet, you can hear her breathing. Stretching out, reaching forth. *Change.* It is coming. Peeking up from beneath the soil, a tender green shoot of possibility and promise, waiting to be nurtured. Do you have room for new growth? Are you able to water and tend to your dreams? Are you able to let light shine upon them? What in your life may be withering from neglect? What has attempted to sprout, but has been cut down, or uprooted, or malnourished?

She's waiting there… in dark spaces. Waiting to uncurl, unfurl, unfold, and *become*. This is a rune of possibility. A rune of deepest wishes. A rune of potential and promise. Something new is taking shape. Something new is waiting to be tended to. Growth happens in dark places. Change grows in dark spaces. **Life**. It is on its way. **Listen**. A seed is calling. What does she need? What do you need? You know.

It is time to dig in the dirt. Time to lie on the earth. Time to soak up the sun and be cleansed by the rain. Time to send down roots and send up shoots.

Put down roots, send up shoots...
Put down roots, send up shoots...

What are you growing?

24: The Tool.

Rune of Labor. Production. Enterprise.

This is a rune of hard work. Satisfying labor. What are you unearthing? What are you digging up? What are you uncovering? What is causing sweat to drip from your brow, your cheeks to flush, and your heart to beat faster? This work can be dirty. It can be long, it can be hard. But, you can do it. You **ARE** doing it. Keep digging.

Remember too that others are doing their own hard work, unearthing their own riches, discovering their own treasures. What might you be missing in other people and how can you work side by side, turning over your deepness together?

This rune helps us recognize the ebb and flow and heave and swell of energy. Life energy. Time. Perspective. There is a time and place for production, for being focused on the *doing* rather than the *being*. There is a time for rest and a time for stillness and the key is recognizing the differences between these times and not **forcing** what is not ready to emerge. Then, when the energy peaks, the shovel comes out and the digging starts. **Go with it.** Put your back into it, lift with your knees, bend with the wind. And, *dig*, sister.

Dig deeply.

25: The Winged Circle.

Rune of Freedom. Liberation. Revolution.

You who carry wholeness within you, spread your wings. It is time to fly. What are you shaking loose? What are you expanding beyond? What are you rising above? Stretch those wings. Feel the quiver of energy pass through them. Feel your feathers drying in the sunlight. Spreading. Opening. Dreaming. Becoming. Lift them up. Test the air. Taste the sweetness of liberation. Take a running start, see the abyss yawning before you, and *soar*.

Soar beyond that which you thought was possible, beyond your capabilities. Soar, knowing that you are carried on a great wind across the sky. While the planet spins, the galaxy swirls, and stars are birthed, you are there, flying on the wings of change and inspiration.

This is a rune of opening. Open opportunity, open possibility. Throw up the shade, draw back the curtains, take down the bars, turn the key, feel the lock click open, and take a running leap.

Liberation. Revolution. Shake off that which you no longer need, and **fly.** Fly free, stand tall, walk true.

Revolution keeps a steady tempo with your heartsong and the color of your wings.

26: The Cauldron of Reflection.

Rune of Solitude. Retreat. Withdrawal. Creative Solitude.

When you draw this rune, you already know what it is you need, what your soul is craving, and what you are asking yourself for over and over and over again. Time to spend alone in your own company. Rest. Reflection. Renewal. Retreat. Pull back, draw in, cocoon. It is time to come into relationship with yourself. To investigate that which you need to know from your own heartspace, your own soulsong.

What is crying out from within you to be heard? What creative impulse wishes to be followed? What heart message longs to be expressed?

It is time to steep in your own knowing. Time to incubate your dreams, creations, and inspirations. Time to merge inner experiencing, to prepare a rich stew, a hearty brew, a precious potion, of your heart's desire. When you draw this rune, *pause.* Rest. Take a time out.

Give yourself permission to take a retreat, to withdraw from external demands, and to sit with yourself:

Savoring your own flavor.

27: The Crowned Heart.

Rune of Unconditional Love. Faith in Love.
Unconditional love.

Open your heart as far as you can, and then, open it just a little further. Run your fingertips lightly over life, stare into its eyes. Breathe deeply, laugh loudly, sing joyously, be wild, be free, be love. If this rune brings up a tight feeling in your chest of *not knowing how*, it is okay, soften into that. Be curious about it. Where does it come from? What are you afraid of? What are you risking? Let your heart be kneaded by Sehkmet's claws until it is soft, pliable, flexible, open.

There is risk in being this vulnerable, this exposed, in letting your heart crack open to your children, to your lover, to your friends, to the world, but it is through the cracks that light enters and transformation is born. Soft, soft. Open, open. Tender, tender. Careful now. *You no longer have to be afraid.*

Love surrounds you and you are an instrument through which its song is played. Make it a sweet one. Make it a long one. Make it a strong one.

28: The Tree.

Rune of Prosperity. Projects. Plant Life. Natural Abundance.

What are you growing? What has taken root and is spreading as your legacy? What rich abundance do you offer to the planet? When you draw this rune, remember all that you *give*. Honor and celebrate that. And, remember all that you have been *given*.

Rest in gratitude and appreciation. The world is a prosperous place. The Earth is an abundant home. In the cycle of giving and receiving, it is possible for each to prosper in their own, healthy way. Stand firmly and feel your roots in deep, solid earth. Giving, receiving. Receiving, giving. In and out. Respiration. Inspiration. Prosperity.

We are the trees of the earth
our roots stretching deep and strong,
the stone of the firmament,
sister to the stars
that gave birth to the soil.

–Alma Villanueva

Lift your arms to the sky and feel sunlight kiss your branches, transforming light to life.

29: The Pentacle.

Rune of Protection. Holding. Maintaining. Sealing. Magic. Five Elements.

Earth, Air, Fire, Water, Spirit. Gather round, circle up. Call the circle, cast the circle, hold the space. It is time to call in the guardians, to ask for help, to protect yourself with the resources that surround you.

Protection. Containment. Safe space. Guard it well, hold it close, create it within yourself and in the environment around you. A circle holds steady. Linked arms are hard to pass through, linked spirits are hard to break.

Don't be afraid to say no, to guard your energy, to guard your safe space within. When you call a circle, let it be guarded: from negative words, pessimistic proclamations, or hurtful stories about others.

Serve as guardian to the terrain within your mind and spirit, as well as in your home, friendships, and circles. You carry protection and safety with you everywhere, whether you may call it up consciously or not, there is still a seal, a container, surrounding your own true self as well.

Earth, Air, Water, Fire, Spirit. Invite them in. Invite them to dance. Revel in the magic of this mystical, embracing union and hold it close to your heart. Guard it with your words, your actions, your thoughts, and your choices.

Every day is sacred.

We walk on holy ground.

30: The Two Circles.

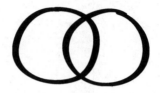

Rune of Merging. Joining or Dividing.

We come together with others in a dance of being so intricate as to be unfathomable. We enter their spheres, they enter ours. Linked, connected, drawing apart. Remaining cells linked forever in the overall body of humanity. Meiosis and mitosis. Separation and connection—always balancing these twin forces.

Recognize when sinking in to another is a thing of holy beauty and recognize when pulling away is the same. Holding hands, linking arms, forming interlocking circles of strength. A chain stretching across time and space, carried lightly on wings of eternity, and nestled, curled and connected in the womb of an ancient mother.

Interdependence cannot be denied. It is essential to survival and strength.

31: The Two Triangles.

Rune of Focus. Analysis. Logic. Rationality.

When you draw this rune, the time has come to be **decisive.** To take action, to be assertive. To choose wisely, but to **choose.** Hone your senses, sharpen your awareness, laser in on that which cries out for your attention. Act with purpose, with determination, without apology. No excuses necessary.

This is rune of clarity and understanding. A rune with clean edges and sharp vision.

You are safe and connected. You are free. Make your choice.

32: Moonboat.

Rune of journeys. Out of body. Astral projection. Travel.

What do I need to know?

She who travels. She who crosses thresholds. She who sets sail for far off places. Journeys can be inner or outer. Journeys can be solitary or communal.

What are you looking for? What are you seeking? To what end do you wish to travel? Do you wish to dig deep into your own soul? Do you wish to adventure across the ocean or into the sisterhood of community?

Now is the time to take that step, to unfurl your sails, and set forth.

33: The Hearth.

Rune of Nurturance. Domesticity. Caring for the Home. Codependency trap.

This is a rune of hearth and home, of caring for one's space as a temple for one's family, of holding space for children and partners. A rune inspiring the creation of rituals and celebrations and ceremony for the members of your closest tribe.

This is a rune of caring, of giving, of sharing, holding, enfolding, rocking, and soothing. This is a rune of love and commitment and attachment. The ties that bind and the bonds of love and blood.

The shadow side of this this rune is the *codependency trap*. Notice when you use your family, your commitment to home and place, as a shield or excuse not to stretch beyond your boundaries, not to extend yourself, not to try, but instead to become complacent.

Be mindful of when you're expecting others to read your mind, be mindful of expecting others to refill your cup for you. Be mindful of trying to continue to pour when your pitcher is empty.

Be careful, be loving, be kind, be open, be brave, be bold.

Link arms with your loved ones and head out smiling into the sunshine and the wide open spaces of shared possibility.

34: The Cauldron of Dancing Women.

Rune of Honor. Loyalty. Commitment.

This is a rune of dedication, of steady purpose, of valor, of showing up, of trying again, of stirring together disparate elements and creating something rich, hearty, and true. This is a stable rune, a sturdy rune, a comfortable, solid, homing rune. It is a rune of sisterhood, of partnership, of community.

Stir with purpose. Cook with passion. Join with grace, ease, and dedication. Make your vows, set your limits, but always be on the lookout for the time to dance. Reach out your hands, join with others, make a vow you will not break: *to be true.* True to your friendships, true to your family, true to your home, and true to yourself.

We all grow within Earth's cauldron. Tempered, forged, mellowed, heated, combined, softened, nourished, transformed.

When you draw this rune, ask yourself: how am I

dancing? To what am I loyal? How am I committing my energy and my love? Do I show up in my own life with honor? Do I walk with commitment? Am I unshakeable in my vows?

This is both a joyful rune and a serious rune. When you link hands with another, do it with great love, great courage, and great commitment.

Be alert for what is bubbling, for what is ready to be served, for what is ready to be savored together.

35: The Broom.

Rune of Purification. Clean sweep. Cleansing.

This is a rune of new beginnings, of starting over, of new possibilities, of sweeping out dusty corners of minds, hearts, and lives. Of flinging open the windows and letting in the sunshine. Of spreading arms in welcome and of laughing with freedom and joy.

Uncover. Turn over. Declutter. Clean sweep. Blank slate. Swipe it away. Clean it out, clear it away. And then, *you're ready.*

With purification comes change and possibility. Hope and power. Peace and freedom. Keep sweeping. Be whole.

What is in the closets or under the beds that needs to be investigated and swept away? What cobwebs are draped from corners of your mind, wound around your heart, laced through your pelvis, twined through your brain, in ways you might not even fully comprehend? What needs to be released, let go, purified, cleansed?

Don't be afraid, pick up your broom and go looking. Turn over all the rocks, look in all the corners, dust down all the cobwebs.

Lay on the earth with your arms spread in the sunshine and know that you are whole. You are loved. You are powerful.

36: The Spiral.

Rune of Initiation. Rites of Passage.

This is a journey rune. Spiraling rites of passage, opened doorways, surrendered moments, grace and struggle in changes, hopeful pauses, liminal places, threshold moments, and leaps of faith.

When this rune is drawn, ask yourself: how have you celebrated transitions? What rites of passage are you preparing for? What initiations are awaiting you? What sacred work calls your name? To what holy purpose will you be dedicated?

Initiation is a path and a process, not a single discrete event. Much like rites of passage mark transitions from one point to another on a continuously unfolding spiral of time, person, and space, one's *whole life* can be a process of initiation. Initiation into your own existence.

Who are you? Who can you be? What holy flame speaks your name? What task ignites your heartsong? What place awaits your visit? What people hunger for your touch?

This is the rune of initiation. This is the rune of change.

It is time for dedication to your sacred path.

37: The Wand.

Rune of Blessing. Making sacred. Honoring. Calling in. Sending forth. Marking boundaries. Consecration. Blessing.

Destiny is knocking and ready to link hands with yours. Pick up your wand, claim your birthright, your power and your destiny. Step out with strength, confidence, and flow. Mark your boundaries without apology or hesitation. Cast the circle, consecrate your heart. Know your body as a temple, your person as an offering, your spirit as a gift.

Cast a circle with your breath. Plant your feet firmly on solid ground and draw up the ancient wisdom that waits for you. Let go of that which holds you back, open wide to embrace that which calls your name, whispering from deep, secret places, from bright, shining spaces, and from quiet corners of your soul.

Name it, bless it, be it, do it, hold it, know it, live it.

It is time to call in that which you need and offer out

that which you have. Giving, receiving, giving, receiving, like the very breaths you take upon this earth. Honor the pulse of blood through your veins, the sparkle of ideas through your mind, the breath filling your lungs, the energy that moves you forward.

Honor, bless, dedicate, consecrate. Hold deep knowing of the inherent worth and value of that which is within you and around you.

Hold yourself, hold the vision, hold the truth, hold the power.

Wave your wand in blessing, in dedication, in honor.

38: The Sun and Moon.

Rune of Laughter. Joy. Ease. Poise. Hilarity. Belly Laughter. Pure Fun. Healing Laughter. Baubo's Rune.

When you draw this rune, take a minute to put down anything else you are carrying, doing, or thinking about. Let your shoulders relax and release. Let the breath move easy down into your belly. Then **smile**. Smile from your roots up through your branches. Feel joy suffuse you, filling you, bathing you, and *laugh*. Laugh from your belly. Laugh from your heart. Laugh with the wild abandon of *freedom* and release.

This is a rune of letting go. This is a rune of release and freedom. This is a rune of trusting oneself and what makes you smile. *Are you afraid to laugh?* Are you scared to let go? Do you fear the loss of control that comes with hilarity? It is time to shake that off. Don't be afraid. Laugh, sister, laugh. It is time to have some *fun!*

Know that you are as free as you allow yourself to be.

39: The Winged Heart.

Rune of Ecstasy. Transcendent state. Peak experience. Orgasm. Psychedelica. Union with all. Awe. Union with Goddess. Out-of-body.

How often do you *think* instead of *feel*? How often do you hold something in your mind rather than feel it in your body? Do you know what ecstasy feels like? Can you allow yourself to experience transcendence, awe, a peak of oneness? Do you know what it is like to have pleasure fill your body, rippling through you and out of your fingertips until you have become a part of the great, seamless, beautiful tapestry that Life is weaving all the time, whether you pay attention or not? Can you spread your arms and sink into the very body of the Goddess?

Close your eyes and let go, melting into her, dissolving control. Releasing, releasing, releasing, until there is nothing left but pure sensation and awe.

Adjust your life, your expectations, and your grasping until ecstasy becomes a regular part of your living and being. This is your birthright, not a one-time treasure, but an awareness to be lived and regularly played with, touched, smelled, tasted, felt.

Dive in. Let it roll over you. Let it sweep you away on the wings of passion and delight.

When this rune is drawn, you know it is not the time for holding on, for standing steady, for grounding, for digging in. It is time for expansion, for ripples of joy to flood you. Time to be swept away, carried away, freed. Flying. Ecstatic. Alive.

It is time to soak your heart in the streams of change, the ocean of possibility, and the arms of All That Is.

There is nothing to lose and everything to gain.

40: The Veil.

Rune of Mystery. Sound of silence. Revealing. Concealing. The Unknown. Not time for answers. The Wishing Rune. Isis Veiled or Unveiled.

What do you see when illusions fall away? When pretensions and old habits crumble to dust? Mystery. Shrouded. Waiting. Concealed. Do you have enough strength to pull back the curtain? Can you gaze into the heart of mystery? To look at what lies in wait. What has been concealed, hidden, put away for so long. What have you hidden? What do you keep concealed? What do you veil from the world?

Some things belong to the sacred mystery, never able to be confronted directly. *Can you hold the space for the ever-unknown as well?* For not knowing. For no answers. Can you hold the hope for that?

What is happening in your inner temple? What remains when everything you don't need has fallen away? What will you see when you drop the curtain and fully examine your own life? What hope waits in shadows? What love is veiled? What are you seeking?

This rune reminds us that sometimes the answers we seek can seem hidden from view. And, that the guidance we seek, the questions we ask, may be met with silence. **Silence is sacred and within it rests infinite possibility.**

Take a deep breath and wait. That which is concealed will be revealed. That which is unknown will become known. That which is unanswered will become answered. And... arising in an endless chain will be new questions, new mysteries, and new possibilities... waiting behind the curtain.

Make a wish. It is time to find your answers in that which is **unknown.**

What is fuzzy, out of focus, distant, shrouded, glazed, covered, secretive, lurking, dancing around the edges of your vision, dancing around the edges of your consciousness, and dancing delicately through your dreams? What is that? What *is that*?

Lift the curtain.

Runing

Daily guidance

The most basic use for Womanrunes is for daily guidance. Sift through the runes or shuffle the cards gently while focusing your thoughts. Take some deep breaths, center yourself in the present moment, and still your mind. When you feel ready, draw a rune and see what it says to you. If you don't recognize the rune automatically, look up its name and then, "let your mind wander around it, and see what associations crop up. Out of this process you should be able to come upon relevant insights that will help to answer your question" (Mountainwater, *Womanrunes* booklet, p. 22). It will also shed light upon issues at hand, whether spoken or unspoken. Another method is to simply open the book at random and see which rune wishes to speak to you.

Drawing a Womanrune as your message or guidepost for the day can be a powerfully centering experience that focuses your thoughts and brings you into clarity for the day to come.

For all runing possibilities included, use your own intuitive understanding first and then draw upon the additional interpretation information in this book.

In Shekhinah's words: "*the main thing to remember with any divination process is that your inner voice knows best. To make contact with this deep part of yourself, it helps to create a ritual setting and make yourself quiet, relaxed, and focused. The more you concentrate on the process, the more successful you will be. **Listening to the deep self is a skill that can be developed like any other...**" (p. 23).*

Multiple types of runing layouts are possible for more elaborate and detailed use. The following section will help you explore some of the many options.

Messages from Womanrunes are not prescriptive or directive, instead they serve as a dynamic conduit to exactly what you need to hear and receive in that moment. When you use them for a longer term question or an annual oracle, remember that they are not intended to *predict* the future, but rather to bring your awareness to themes, issues, or messages that are calling for your attention.

Three rune basic spread

After following the initial basic centering process, draw three runes and lay them out in a row. The first rune represents the past and its relationship to your current issue or question. The second represents the present. The third represents the future and what you need to know as you move forward.

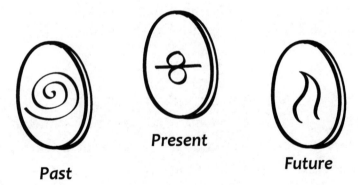

Past

Present

Future

The Crone Throw

This layout is based on one described in the book Crone Stones by Carol Lee Campbell (www.cronestones.com).

After focusing your thoughts and centering your body and breath, choose three runes and lay them out left to right.

The first rune is the **Maiden** rune. *It reveals your potential in the situation.*

The second rune is the **Mother** rune. *It tells your outcome to the situation.*

The third rune is the **Crone** rune. *It is your explanation of how to achieve the first two runes.*

(Crone Stones manual, p. 67)

Maiden

Mother

Crone

Shekhinah's Layout

(reprinted from the original Womanrunes booklet, p. 25)

Meanings:

1. **Self:** identity, personality, self-image, current feelings, attitudes, situations.
2. **Relationships:** love matters, interaction, intimacy, partnerships, family, friends.
3. **Environment:** living space, workspace, surroundings and their influences.
4. **Immediate past:** recent occurrences and energies.
5. **Immediate future:** upcoming occurrences and energies.
6. **Healing:** health matters, sources of healing, what needs healing.
7. **Livelihood:** career, money, survival, work.
8. **Deep past:** childhood, long-range past, past lives, roots of personality.
9. **Wild rune:** random energy, surprises, possibilities, tendencies.
10. **Magic:** spirituality, religion, psychic matters, the soul's journey.
11. **Change:** influences of and for change, transformations; that which is changing.
12. **Wish rune:** hopes, dreams, expectations, projections, fears.
13. **Outcome:** probable future, culmination of the runes.

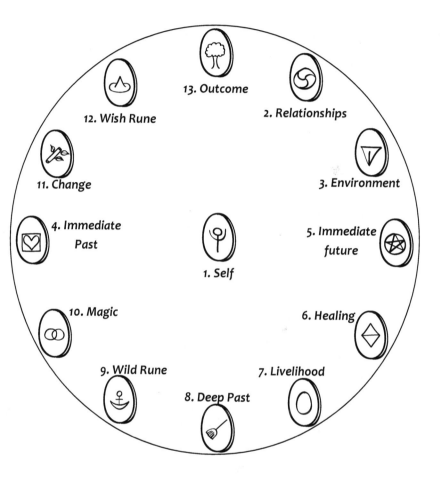

13. Outcome

12. Wish Rune

2. Relationships

11. Change

3. Environment

4. Immediate Past

1. Self

5. Immediate future

10. Magic

6. Healing

9. Wild Rune

7. Livelihood

8. Deep Past

Goddess Guidance layout

(adapted from a method in *The Goddess Speaks* by Dee Poth, p. 8-9)

After centering, draw six runes at random and lay them out in a two-three-one arrangement (see illustration). The first two runes deal with the outer and this is where you will bring your question, issue, or concern. The second line of three runes represents your inner direction and may involve your inner, deep response or knowing about your question. The final row with one rune suggests the action to be taken or outcome to be pursued.

Row 1: Question or situation you bring to the Goddess

Row 2: Inner response and Goddess guidance.

Row 3: Action to take.

Action Spread

(adapted from my favorite tarot deck, The Gaian Tarot by Joanna Powell Colbert, p. 252. http://www.gaiantarot.com/)

With a specific situation or issue in mind that needs action, draw four runes and lay out in the order illustrated below. Make sure to specify the timeline—are you looking at two weeks, one month, three months, six months, one year for resolution or insight?

1.   **Now:** *what's going on? Present energies or circumstances or your topic or situation.*
2.   **Helpful action:** *Things appropriate to do or embody in this situation. Positive doable steps. This might relate to helpful people, situations, or opportunities.*
3.   **What to avoid:** *Things that would not be helpful or constructive. What not to do. May also illustrate people, situations, or events that could be unhelpful.*
4.   **Most likely outcome:** *guidance on resolution or completion of the situation or issue.*

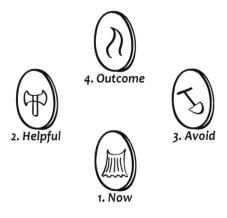

4. Outcome

2. Helpful

3. Avoid

1. Now

Annual oracle

In January of the new year, set aside some time, energy, and focused ritual space to draw an annual oracle for yourself for the year to come. Draw 12 runes and lay them out, one for each month of the year. Record the symbols and their basic message on a grid for an overview of the upcoming year. Refer to the grid for ongoing guidance throughout the year.

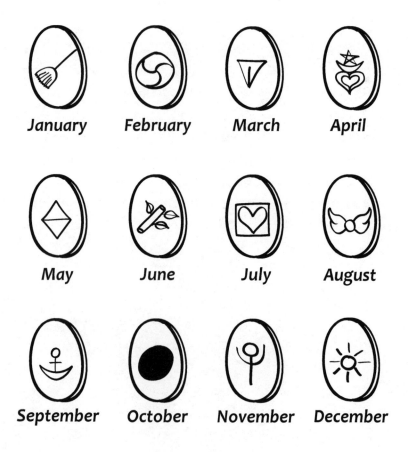

January   February   March   April

May   June   July   August

September   October   November   December

Annual oracle variation

(adapted from my favorite tarot deck, The Gaian Tarot by Joanna Powell Colbert, p. 262. http://www.gaiantarot.com/)

Draw seven runes at the beginning of the new year and lay out as illustrated. As with other layouts, take a few moments to sit with the entire layout and intuit its overall pattern and message before moving on to specific interpretations. Basic correspondences for this layout are as follows:

1. What do I leave behind in the old year?

2. What do I open up to in the new year?

3. Key opportunity of the new year.

4. Key challenge of the new year.

5. Hidden concern (this rune should be pulled from the bottom of the deck).

6. Deep wisdom/advice from goddess.

7. Key theme of the new year.

If you keep a record from year to year, the following year use the last rune from the preceding year (7) as the first rune in the next year's layout.

1. Leave behind   2. Open up   3. Opportunity   4. Challenge

5. Hidden concern   6. Deep wisdom   7. Key theme

How to make your own Womanrunes

There are many ways to make your own set of
Womanrunes. I suggest making several different
kinds of sets to serve different purposes or settings.
A basic means is to etch each symbol on a disk of
polymer clay, self-hardening clay, oven-hardening
clay, or pottery clay (later fired in a kiln).

An even simpler method is to use permanent
markers to draw each Womanrune on a pebble, a
beach rock, or a wooden circle.

Another simple method is to draw each symbol on
card stock or small index cards. Write the name of
each rune beneath the symbol for easy reference for
divination.

You may use glass paint markers to draw each rune
on a glass pebbles from a craft store or pet store
(often sold as material for aquariums). The paint is
then fired in your kitchen oven and becomes
resistant to scratching.

Using permanent markers to draw each rune on
small squares of fabric is another easy possibility.
You might also choose to embroider the
Womanrunes on fabric squares.

Other uses

Prayer flag set

One of my very favorite additional uses for Womanrunes was brought to our women's circle by a friend. Using white fabric and permanent markers, we each made a set of small "prayer flag" style Womanrunes. With the top of each square folded over about ½ inch and sewn (ends left open), the flags may then be chosen at random or with intentional purpose to send a specific message or attract a specific aspect. Slide the flags onto a wooden dowel and then place in the ground or into a deck post or porch rail. I change my series of flags regularly and enjoy seeing their messages flutter in the breeze on my front porch.

Calamoondala

Each year I have a tradition of drawing a circular mandala moon calendar for the upcoming year. I use black paper and white colored pencils and map out the dates of the full and new moons for the coming year. I choose a Womanrune for each moon (some years using random selection, some years using conscious intention to attract or manifest) and draw the symbols on my Calamoonndala.

Runewriting

One of Shekhinah's purposes in creating the Womanrunes was to create a woman-identified alphabet writing system. On the original pronunciation guide included in this book (p. 126), you will find the correspondences between each Womanrune and the English language. You may use runewriting to write your own name or to write messages on cards to your friends. I've used runewriting with my family to create pocket totems for power, courage, and inspiration as well.

Sample

Rune

Writing

Bindrunes

A bindrune is a new rune created purposefully through the combination of several runes. These runes are "bound" together or combined to give additional meanings or symbols. You can create a bindrune of your own name or other word or concept.

The name Brigid in runewriting

Runewritten Brigid combined into a bindrune.

Runespells

Combining related Womanrunes into bindrunes can also create a runespell. For example:

Will   Power   Willpower

"Runespells can be done in a number of ways. A single rune can be used as an affirmation to bring desired results. The Love Rune, for example, can be used to bring or strengthen love. Draw it on a piece of paper and place it in a magical pouch on your altar. Etch or paint it on a special stone; rose quartz for example…" (Womanrunes booklet, p. 17).

You may also make runesigns over things you wish to bless or infuse with runic meaning or power.

Pocket Totem

Using polymer clay or another sculpting medium, create a round disk. Onto the surface of the disk, etch your name in Womanrunes as well as other runes that you wish to attract, remember, or learn from. Fire or bake the clay and then carry the totem close to you as a reminder of your own power, potential, and purpose.

In PMH Atwater's book, *Runes of the Goddess*, she explains:

Indeed, long before there was ever a need for hieroglyphic script, there must have been a desire and a passion for recreating patterns in the mind that would evoke the immediacy of special moments. These special moments would have been no less than ones where earth and sky, heaven and human, seemed to merge, intermingling the invisible with the visible. Such would have been times of awe and wonder... when spirit reigned.

These patterns in the mind would have quickly become anchored in collective memory because of their connection to basic comprehension levels and survival urges...

These patterns in the mind are the real runes.

(Atwater, p. 135)

May these Womanrunes help you understand the richness of your own mind, the depth of your own intuition, and the power and potentiality of the vast Womanspirit that enfolds us all.

0. ◯ The Circle
Rune of Self

1. ⌂ The Witches' Hat
Rune of Magic

2. ☾ The Crescent Moon
Rune of Divination

3. ▽ The Yoni
Rune of Making

4. ♫ The Flame
Rune of Fire

5. ♡ The Heart
Rune of Love

6. ⚒ The Labyris
Rune of Will

7. ♀ The Dancing Woman
Rune of Power

8. ☐ The Box, Rune of
Limitation

9. ● The Dark Moon
Rune of Wisdom

10. ☯ The Wheel
Rune of Fate

11. ↗ The Pendulum
Rune of Karma

12. 8 The Reflection
Rune of Surrender

13. ⚥ The Flying Woman
Rune of
Transformation

14. ♨ The Cauldron
Rune of Alchemy

15. ◐ The Whole Moon
Rune of Psyche

16. ૭ The Serpent, Rune
of Awakening

17. ☪ The Moon & Star
Rune of Faith

18. ☼ The Sun
Rune of Healing

19. ⚘⚘ The Dancing Women
Rune of Celebration

20. ⟲ The Great Wheel
Rune of Infinity

21. ◊ The Egg
Rune of Naming

22. ♀♀ The Sisters
Rune of Friendship

23. ♀ The Seed
Rune of Waiting

24. ↓ The Tool
Rune of Labor

25. ✶ The Winged Circle
Rune of Freedom

26. ♨ The Cauldron of
Reflection
Rune of Solitude

27. ♕ The Crowned Heart
Rune of Compassion

28. 🌳 The Tree
Rune of Prosperity

29. ⛤ The Pentacle
Rune of Protection

30. ◑ The Two Circles
Rune of Merging

31. ◇ The Two Triangles
Rune of Focus

32. ⚓ The Moonboat
Rune of Journeys

33. ❤ The Hearth, Rune
of Nurturance

34. ♨ The Cauldron of
Dancing Women
Rune of Honor

35. ✦ The Broom, Rune of
Purification

36. ◉ The Spiral
Rune of Initiation

37. ⚸ The Wand
Rune of Blessing

38. ☼ The Sun & Moon
Rune of Laughter

39. ♥ The Winged Heart
Rune of Ecstasy

⌒ The Veil
Rune of Mystery

O – with voice
θ – without voice

WOMANRUNES ©
Pronunciation Guide

0. ◯ "I" as in h**i**gh

1. △ "W" as in **w**itch

2. ℂ "L" as in **l**ove

3. ▽ "M" as in **m**other

4. ◖ "R" as in **r**oar

5. ♡ "AH" as in m**a**ma

6. ⋈ "B" as in **b**ig / "P" as in **p**ush

7. ⴲ "ŏŏ" as in b**oo**k

8. ▢ "ng" as in wi**ng**

9. ● "J" as in **j**ay / "ch" as in **ch**ild

10. ⟠ "ĭ" as in **i**t

11. ⌐ "ă" as in **a**t

12. ⴲ "ŭ" as in **u**p (the bending vowel)

13. ⋎ "N" as in **n**ow

14. ⊟ "ĕ" as in w**e**t

15. ◯ "ēē" as in s**ee**

16. ⧓ "ss" as in **s**a**ss**y / "zz" as in **z**oo

17. ⊌ "ōō" as in s**oo**n

18. ⊙ "aw" as in s**aw**

19. ⊙⊙ "Y" as in **y**es

20. ⊂⊃ "ō" as in sl**ow**

21. ◯ "h" as in **h**ome

22. ∏∏ "K" as in **k**iss / "G" as in **g**ood

23. ⏃ "sh" as in **sh**e / "zh" as in vi**s**ion

24. ⎛ "F" as in **f**ine / "V" as in **v**ote

25. ⌣ "Th" as in **th**ick / "th" as in **th**en

26. ⊗ "ea" as in b**ea**r

27. ⧆ "au" as in n**ow**

28. ⚘ "T" as in **T**ipi / "D" as in **d**og

29. ⛤ "Ā" as in st**ay**

30. ⊘ African click

31. ⬡ Welsh/German/Hebrew guttural "ckh"

32. ⚓ French "R"

33. ⬙ French nasal as in "sa**ns**"

34. ⊎ "ě" as in h**er**

35. ⟍ Rolled "R" rrrrr

36. ◎ "wh" as in **wh**ere

37. ⴼ "ua" as in K**ore**

38. ↜ Gasping – the indrawn breath

39. ⊙ "oi" as in **oy** vay

⬙ Silence

PLEASE KEEP SYSTEM INTACT

©1988 Shekhinah Mountainwater
New edition Jan. 2001
Please use and acknowledge

Shakti Woman Speaks

Shakti woman speaks.
She says Dance
Write
Create
Share
Speak.
Don't let me down.
I wait within
coiled at the base of your spine,
draped around your hips
like a bellydancer's sash,
snaking my way up
through your belly
and your throat
until I burst forth
in radiant power
that shall not be denied.
Do not silence me.
Do not coil my energy back inside
stuffing it down
where it might wither in darkness
biding its time
becoming something that waits
to strike.
Let me sing.
Let me flood through your body
in ripples of ecstasy.
Stretch your hands wide,
wear jewels on your fingers
and your heart on your sleeve.
Spin.
Spin with me now
until we dance shadows into art
hope into being
and pain into power.

About the author

Molly is a priestess, writer, teacher, and artist who lives with her husband and children in the Midwest. She is a doctoral student in women's spirituality at Ocean Seminary College and a professor of human services. She holds master's degrees in both clinical social work and in goddess studies. Molly and her husband co-create at Brigid's Grove: http:// brigidsgrove.com and she blogs about theapoetics, ecopsychology, and the Goddess at http:// goddesspriestess.com.

Acknowledgments

Shekhinah Mountainwater for the very idea, the symbols, and the beginnings.

Joy Harjo in the anthology *Open Mind* for the phrase "night wind woman" (used in opening poem).

Anne Key for the image of the heart kneaded by Sekhmet's claws (in *Desert Priestess: A Memoir*).

SageWoman Magazine (www.sagewoman.com) for sparking my curiosity about Womanrunes more than 24 years after actually publishing the article!

Global Goddess (www.globalgoddess.org) email list for additional information about Womanrunes and for helping me excavate old information from the depths of the internet.

Karen Orozco for author photograph, p. 129.

Phanie Stuckey for the prayer flags.

Amy Terrill and Shellei Kittrell for *showing up*.

Mark Remer for love and for looking outward in the same direction.

Barbara and Tom Johnson for everything.

Resources

Ariadne's Thread by Shekhinah Mountainwater available used from online booksellers (plus her little booklet *Womanrunes*, sometimes available from: http://shekhinah.net/)

Crone Stones by Carol Lee Campbell. Available from www.cronestones.com. I absolutely *love* this set and the book that goes with it. Extremely powerful.

The Gaian Tarot by Joanna Colbert. My very favorite tarot deck. Earth-honoring, insightful, beautiful, and practical. http://www.gaiantarot.com/

The Goddess Speaks oracle deck and accompanying book by Dee Poth (available from used booksellers).

Runes of the Goddess by PMH Atwater (http://pmhatwater.hypermart.net/).

Free Introduction to Womanrunes Class:

http://mysteryschoolofthegoddess.com/courses/175/about

Come join the Circle!

Our Creative Spirit Circle is free and packed with beautiful, bountiful resources, including a free Womanrunes e-course, Red Tent materials, birth blessing posters, access to Divine Imperfections sculptures at 50% off, and more. It also includes our weekly newsletter filled with resources such as ceremony outlines, card layouts, articles, sneak peeks, and special freebies. Claim your place in the Circle: brigidsgrove.com/come-join-the-circle

Connect with Brigid's Grove

Molly and Mark co-create original goddess sculptures, pendants, birth art, and ceremony kits at http://brigidsgrove.etsy.com. They publish *Womanrunes* book and deck sets, as well as *The Red Tent Resource Kit*, *The Ritual Recipe Kit*, and *Earthprayer, Birthprayer, Lifeprayer, Womanprayer*.

There are many ways to keep up with our projects, programs, books, art, and family.

- brigidsgrove.com
- facebook.com/brigidsgrove
- instagram.com/brigidsgrove
- brigidsgrove.etsy.com
- twitter.com/brigidsgrove
- Creative Spirit Circle FB Group: facebook.com/groups/creativeceremonyacademy

Also from Brigid's Grove

Inspiring online courses and circle subscriptions

- Womanrunes Immersion
- Red Tent Initiation Program
- Practical Priestessing
- Divination Practicum
- Creating Women's Circles
- Womanspirit Initiation
- Priestess Path + Priestess Workbook
- Family Magic
- Goddess Magic
- Seasonal Ceremonies

Womanrunes Immersion e-course

This 41 day e-course takes you on a deep personal journey, uncovering your inner wisdom and deep truth using *Womanrunes*, a powerful system of divination and intuitive guidance for personal growth. Used as a dynamic, hands-on, participatory system, Womanrunes become part of your own *language* of the Divine, the Goddess, your inner wisdom, and womanspirit truths.

Molly also offers a 7 week Divination Practicum online.

www.brigidsgrove.com